Francis William Bourdillon

Miniscula

Lyrics of Nature, Art and Love

Francis William Bourdillon

Miniscula

Lyrics of Nature, Art and Love

ISBN/EAN: 9783744776288

Printed in Europe, USA, Canada, Australia, Japan

Cover: Foto ©Thomas Meinert / pixelio.de

More available books at **www.hansebooks.com**

Minuscula

Lyrics of Nature, Art and Love

By
Francis William Bourdillon

London : Lawrence & Bullen, Ltd.
16 Henrietta Street, Covent Garden
MDCCCXCVII

The poems contained in this little volume are for the most part the siftings of three yet smaller volumes of verse, published anonymously at Oxford in 1891, 1892, and 1894, and now withdrawn from sale. But I have added certain new poems, which in the Contents are marked with an asterisk, besides four which appeared in the American edition of *Ailes d'Alouette*.

CONTENTS

Part I. Art and Nature

	PAGE
THE SHELLEY MEMORIAL	3
AN ARTIST'S LITANY	8
WHEN MUSIC DIES	10
*JOY'S WAY	11
*TO A LARK	12
QUEEN SPRING	13
MAYTIME	15
AN ENGLISH EDEN	16
AN AUTUMN SONG	17
AUTUMN SINGERS	18
*CORYDALIS	19
CATCHWORDS	20
FOUND DROWNED	21
THE MYRIAD-MOTHER	22
AT EVEN	23
WINGED ANTS	24

	PAGE
*The Lodestar	25
In a Cage	26
Poeta atque Navis	27
Shadows	28
The Sinner	29

Part II. Love

	PAGE
*Love's Largesse	33
*Life and Love	34
Mother-of-Pearl	35
The Words of Lovers	36
Darkening Years	37
A Rippled Stone	38
Two Dreams	39
A Butterfly on a Glacier	40
After their Year	41
"Where all Love's Pilgrims come"	42
Star-Glimpses	43
Vibrations	44
A Day of Love	45
*What is Love but a Dreamer?	46
*The Song-Master	47
*The Herald-Flower	48
Lost Leaves of the Greek Anthology	49

Part III. Man's Love

	PAGE
IN INFERNO SUSTULIT OCULOS	55
IN EXITU AMORIS	56
*CYNTHIA	57
A SONG OF FAREWELL	58
A LOVE-SONG	59
OMENS AND DREAMS	60
*THE AFTERGLOW	61
ILLUMINATION	62
VISA MIHI VERITAS	63
*THE WORD AFTER FAREWELL	64
TOGETHER, ONCE	65
OUTRE-MER	66
KISSES	67
ASK OF THE NIGHTINGALE	68
A SONG OF LOVE	69
*A SILVER NIGHT	70
EHEU, FUGACES!	71
A SUMMER CLOUD	72
A FALLEN IDOL	73
*ANY MAN TO ANY WOMAN	74
A MAN'S QUESTION	75
THE BIRD AND THE BEACON	76
THE STORY OF A LOVER'S SOUL	77

	PAGE
The Poisoned Butterfly	79
Finis sine Fine	80
The Happy Spring	81
The One Day	82
The Magic Maiden	83
A Magic Circle	84
Earth has Forgotten	85
Via Invia	86
A Rondel of the Ivy-Leaf	87
A Rondel of Absence	88
Love Sonnets	89

Part IV.   Maiden's Love

The Story of the Rose	97
To-day He Loves Me	98
"Si vous croyez que je vais dire"	99
Ce que vivent les Roses	100
I and You	101
A Woman's Question	102
Not in Naxos	103
A Story heard on a Violin	105
A Revolt	106
Planctus Displicentis	107

Part I
Art and Nature

The Shelley Memorial

(in University College, Oxford)

Itaque testimonio estis vobismet ipsis : quod filii estis
 eorum qui prophetas occiderunt.

THIS is not Shelley—this dead mask of Death !
 Here is no marble Immortality,
But fleshly petrifaction. Could the breath
 Come back to this, yet nevermore should he,
The stately spirit of full stature, deign
In this small corpse to lodge, and live again.

This is not Shelley ! Have our eyes not seen
 Shelley, the child of morning, with the light
Of Heaven about him, and a brow serene
 As Orient noonday, smile on Death and Night,
As the unhappy sisters of man's sorrow,
That might not live to the bright human morrow ?

This marble but records Death's victory
   In Death's own lying language ; who doth
      boast
That o'er all Being he hath empery,
   And nothing liveth when the breath is lost.
So cold, so white, he cries, your Shelley lay !
Such lifeless limbs ! Such heavy soul-less clay !

Where is his Immortality—ah, where ?
   Is this the sky of Shelley ? These his stars ?
This small blue dome, as low, as near, as bare
   As infant man believed it, and these sparse
Gold spangles ! Could ye mock our Shelley
      more
'Twixt him and Heav'n than draw this tinsel
      o'er ?

Yet who here standing blames the sculptor's
      art ?
   So deftly moulded is each marble limb !
Such deathly languor lies on every part !
   So like is this to what was left of him,
When the wave-wantons, tiring of a prey
Teased vainly, flung the emptied flesh away !

Not his the fault, the sculptor's! Is it ours,
  Who leave no more to Art her old domain
Of Fancy, and though sky and sea she scours,
  No more allow her to present us plain
Her aery visions, or to unseen things
Lend bodies visible and birdlike wings?

She bears Egyptian bondage, set to make
  No likeness but what workman souls may see
And test by finger-touch—the fowler's lake,
  The fisher's river-side, the woodman's tree,
The face in soul-less hours of common life,
The body naked for the surgeon's knife.

Where are her ancient glories, when to man
  She brought a revelation all divine,
And opened his dull eyes, and bade him scan
  Shy Nature, to discern why she did shine,
For all her sorrows, with so calm a light;
And, through the outward, woke the inward sight?

Here had the Greek made plain in mortal
    form
  The seed of the Immortals, the half-god ;
Here had the Florentine shewn flesh all warm
    With mystic fire-tints from the Rose of
    God ;
The rudest missal-scribe, his rough child-way,
Had drawn the soul-shape 'scaping from
    the clay.

We only, lords of lightning and of light,
  All Nature's magic working to our wand,
Are yet forbidden the most simple sight
  Of the informing soul in sea or land,
In hills and clouds and the blue deeps above,
And woman's beauty, and the face we love.

One was there, son of England, whom not yet
  The dust of years hides deeply, who per-
    chance
With visionary touch had made forget
  This dead marred body, left but to enhance
The bright miraculous likeness upward drawn,
The unprisoned spirit springing to the Dawn.

But Blake, the last Prometheus, is no more,
  And the dark Heaven has shut her gates
    again.
Turn to the sleeper here, if in the lore
  He left us we may find some balm for
    pain,
May find him living, though this gray-hued
  Death
So grimly to his dying witnesseth.

There do we find him, with his young-god's
  face
  For ever to the East—for ever sure
Of the delaying sunrise, and the grace
  To dawn upon the dark earth, full and
    pure
And holy, though a hundred such as he
Should die in faith before that day shall be.

An Artist's Litany

WISDOM to others—to see
    Thy face and live ;
But the hunger of Beauty to me,
    Good Father, give !

In Earth and Heaven to know
    Transfiguring light :
To drink of the sunset glow
    With the inward sight :

The glory of Heaven to learn
    From a wayside weed :
The Eden of God to discern
    In a daisied mead :

To look through lustrous eyes
    To the soul of a girl,
And covet no selfish prize
    Of casquet or pearl :

Crown of the Maker's craft,
    The white-limbed Eve,
To worship, and no warm waft
    Of the flesh receive!

Wisdom to others—to see
    Thy face and live:
But the hunger of Beauty to me,
    Good Father, give!

When Music Dies

The doors of Eden close
   When music dies.
The odours of the rose,
   The warm wind's sighs—

Ev'n as a dream they fade:
   The dew-washed feet
Pass from the cedarn shade
   To sands and heat.

Joy's Way

SKIMMING an idle stone along the lake
    An idle day,
Sudden I saw a little rainbow wake
    Among the spray,
Which, trying oft, I could no more remake.

    This is Joy's way!
All in a moment on our eyes to break,
    Then flee away,
Nor all our labour e'er can bring it back,
    Nor all our play.

To a Lark

O LITTLE singing bird,
If I could word
In as sweet human phrase
Thy hymn of praise,

The world should hearken me
As I do thee,
And I should heed no more
Than thou, but soar!

Queen Spring

I MET Queen Spring in the Hanger
    That slopes to the river gray;
Yestreen the thrushes sang her,
    But she came herself to-day.

She is fair as a mortal maiden;
    But all I saw was the clouds
With a new refulgence laden
    As they drifted by in crowds.

Her voice is sweet as a viol;
    But all I heard was the song
Of the blackbird making trial
    If yet his notes were strong.

Her touch is soft as the water;
    But all I felt was the kiss
Of the warm South wind that had brought her
    On those wide wings of his.

Her breath is sweet as the showers ;
  But all I caught was the scent
Of her sacred primrose flowers
  Flinging incense where she went.

For so do the things diviner
  Come within human ken,
Through some perception finer
  Than the fivefold senses of men.

Maytime

Oh, the Maytime
Is the playtime!
Petals falling,
Cuckoos calling,
   Here and there;
Flowers springing
Wood-birds singing
   Everywhere.

Oh, the woodland
Is the good land!
All that rare is
In Maytime there is.

In sweet places
   Children's features
Take the graces
   Of wild creatures,
Till their faces
Gleam and dimple
With the simple
   Look of flowers;
And their brightening
Is the enlightening
   Of dark hours.

An English Eden

Roses drop their petals all around
    In that enchanted ground,
And all the air is murmurous with sound
    From the white-tumbling weir;
So that all lesser voices heard anear
    Do half unreal appear.

As one half-waking from a dreamless sleep,
    Is fain his thought to keep,
Thus floating ever 'twixt the night's black deep
    And the blank glare of day;
So in that Eden pauses life half-way
    'Twixt dawning and full day.

An Autumn Song

Lay by, sweet woodlands, your array
    Of gold and green !
How should ye wear it in the day
    When Spring, your Queen,
    Is chased away
By rebels from her bright demesne ?

Farewell, delight of lustrous leaves
    And shining flowers !
Many an unseen hand unweaves
    The royal bowers.
    Earth's self receives
Sullenly the usurping Powers.

Autumn Singers

WHEN woods are gold and hedges gay
With jewelled Autumn's brief array,
And diamonds sprinkle every spray,
    The robin sings
His soft melodious well-a-day
    For dying things.

Yet often, when a riotous night
Has ruined half the wood's delight,
There breaks a Spring day, warm and
    bright,
    And the thrush sings,
As though his April were in sight,
    Of quickening things.

Corydalis

THERE is a little plant that weaves
About the withered gorse its leaves
    Upon the Malvern Hills;
And lifts a tiny tuft of flowers,
To take the sunshine and the showers,
    The heats and dewy chills.

We may not think a soul is there,
Nor courage, though it seems to dare
    The rains, the early snows;
Nor patience, though so late it clings,
Nor pity for unhappier things,
    Though round rough stems it grows.

Nor any joy to be admired,
Nor soft desire to be desired,
    Although so fair it be.
Yet, gentle maid, I pray thee make
A parable hereof, and take
    This fable unto thee!

Catchwords

Though joy and grief and pain
    More fast our memories bleach
Than sun and wind and rain
    The fall'n leaves of the beech:

Yet what light things remain!
    Some look, some little speech,
Remembered, brings again
    His life's great hour to each.

Found Drowned

The sigh of the sea-wind wakes not
  The dead in the deep :
The lapse of the light wave breaks not
  Their dreamless sleep.

Nor the sorrow of those that loved them,
  Nor the love of the loved, again
Can make this thing that the light waves fling
  A creature of joy and pain.

The Myriad-Mother

THE storm is dying with the day,
And crimson fringes fret the gray;
The shifting clouds show lakes of blue,
And in the West the sun looks through.

Listen, through all the woods is plain
The music of melodious rain,
And from the oak the blackbird's psalm
Hushes the weeping woods to calm.

O Nature, whom thy children trust,
Mother of myriads, it is just!
My grief has had thy tears awhile;
Smile now for others who can smile!

At Even

O TOILERS of the day!
How, when the even-calm
Droppeth like sweetest balm
Upon your weary brows, can ye not
    pray?
But nay!
Some to the hot play-house,
Some to the rank carouse,
Forgetting God, ye go astray.
And all the while above,
The lamps of heavenly love,
The shining stars, show the more
    excellent way.

Winged Ants

THESE little crawling ants for one day's space
  Had Iris-wings of gossamer, and flew,
Light as the down of thistles, in the face
    Of smiling heaven, whose frown not yet
      they knew.
  The world was all a wonder, green and
    blue ;
And light the labour down soft winds to race,
Ere yet they learned earth's dust to be their
    place,
  Toil their inheritance, and death their due.

O human toilers ! though no good ye know
  But labour, and no certain goal but death,
    Was not your youth in dreams iridian
      dressed ?
Why will ye those bright memories forgo,
  Nor list again your childhood's lore, which
    saith,
    Not life laborious, but life winged, is
      best ?

The Lodestar

What shipmen steering by yon star
  ·What separate ports have gained !
What climes, what seas, what havens far
  By that one guide attained !

So shines the unreached Heavenly Light
  To every seeking soul,
And guides each several seeker right
  Unto his several goal.

In a Cage

O HEART, what boots thy wild wing-beating
    At prison bars?
To thee the hope of flowers is cheating
    As hope of stars.

What sadness can the sunlight bring thee,
    The air so mild?
What sorrow can the blithe birds sing thee
    To weep so wild?

Alas! the Spring is in all places,
    And soft the air;
The woods are bright with primrose faces,
    And I not there!

Poeta atque Navis

POETA. Art thou, poor wave-beat hull, the same
We watched amid the port's acclaim
Receive on wreathèd prow thy name?

Poor ship! How hard have dealt with thee
The fortunes of the wind and sea,
Who seemed for fairer fate to be!

NAVIS. And thou, poor world-sick soul, art thou
The same on whose unwrinkled brow
Was set for crown the laurel bough?

Now have I rest from wind and wave:
But thou hast still the storms to brave
Of life whose haven is the grave.

Shadows

Most strange it is to stand when shades are free—
  Loosed from the light that chained them here and there,
  To hold their hushed dominion everywhere—
To stand and commune with them silently.
  For one was bound by daylight's tyrant glare
The faithful follower of a cur to be;
And one was forced—light fetters needed he—
  To wait all day upon a maiden fair.

And each wore then the shape of love or loathing
  Of him whom Day their daylong master made;
Now all have doffed their loved or hated clothing,
  And mingle o'er the earth in shapeless shade.
And we, when Death shall lose our souls from Self,
Shall shudder to have served so foul an elf.

The Sinner

I saw one crouching in a place of gloom,
  Loaded with chains, abject and miserable.
A prayer broke from him : suddenly the room
  Lightened, and lo, an angel veritable
    Straight from God's presence. Th' iron ponderable
Shrivelled like web-work of Arachne's loom ;
He stretched his limbs, he changed that living tomb
  For space and light and airs esperitable.

I saw him kneeling, weeping praise to God.
  I looked again : the prisoner, lately free,
    Of his own will had entered that dark door
    Again—again his limbs the fetters wore
By his own will. O Jesu ! can Thy blood,
  Can all the might of Heaven save him, or me ?

Part II

Love

Love's Largesse

The heaven has emptied all her stars
    Into the glimmering sea ;
Yet in yon skies the lifted eyes
    Find not one less to be.

So Love gives all ; and lo, the hand
    Emptied, the head stripped bare,
Are ringed and crowned more richly round
    With jewels yet more rare.

Life and Love

Bright is that wave of night
With a happy tremulous light
On whose wide-wandering breast
One wavering star doth rest.

Till the night-wind dies away,
And the star fades out in the day,
And the wave sinks down to sleep
Unknown in the heaving deep.

Mother-of-Pearl

Not from all shells in Indian bays
    Are pearls to win ;
Nor hath the gentle heart always
    A love within.

But where the pearl hath lain, the shell
    Shows yet the sheen ;
And there's a soul-look that doth tell
    Where love hath been.

The Words of Lovers

The sweetest words that tongue has said,
    Or songs that lips have sung,
Are sad with thoughts of lovers dead,
    And many a silent tongue;

Yet faintly fragrant as perfume
    Which age on age has lain
In sepulchres of scented gloom,
    Now used of men again.

Darkening Years

Love drinks our young sorrows up,
    As the light
Exhaleth from the blossom-cup
    The dews of night.

Alas, the day when grief grows stronger
    In darkening years!
Alas, the day when love no longer
    Can dry our tears!

A Rippled Stone

Sands, forsaken, keep
    The impress of sea-kisses;
As lovers' lips in sleep
    Repeat the day's caresses.

And often hearts hard-grown,
    Deep-hidden and discerned not,
Have kept the tale in stone
    Of love-tides that returned not.

Two Dreams

A DREAM of light !—
   A sunlit sea
Melting in bright
   Infinity.
O Light ! O Love !
   For ever and evermore !

A dream of night !—
   A stream's dark flow ;
Glimmering white
   Of chillest snow.
O Night ! O Death !
   For ever and evermore !

A Butterfly on a Glacier

The wind blows warm from Italy
    Across the wastes of snow ;
And thou, poor bright-winged butterfly,
    Dreamedst—how shouldst thou know ?—
To follow the delicious breeze
To new strange flowers on honied leas.

So, wind of Love, thou whisperest
    Of warm, enchanted lands ;
And lur'st the heart to leave its rest
    And follow Love's commands ;
Then leav'st it, as the butterfly,
Alone in icy wastes to die.

After their Year

How lightly waver down through slanting beams
    The leaves grown sere!
Ev'n so unheeded fall Love's faded dreams
    After their year.

But oh! the green leaf, and the living love!
    Storms rend the sky,
And light is darkened in the heaven above
    If these must die.

"Where all Love's Pilgrims come"

THIS is the grave of Love,
    By tears kept green.
We know he is dead, sweet Love,
    So long unseen.

And this is his grave, we know;
    For here in Spring
The first blue violets blow,
    The first birds sing.

Star-Glimpses

When the night-wind stirs the pine,
Comes and goes the sweet star-shine
Through the boughs—a soul divine.

When love breathes, the deeps of being
Dazzle suddenly our seeing,
Like a star through dark boughs fleeing.

Vibrations

What wonder if, when Love awakes
Suddenly, the tense heart breaks !
As at the organ's thundering
Snaps the lute's responsive string.

Ah, sadder heart, where Love has grown
Stealthily, his name unknown !
As at some wandering noiseless air
The wind-harp wakens to despair.

A Day of Love

Dear is the sunny between-while
    Of April skies,
Though black with storm in the meanwhile
    The clouds arise.

Tho' the clouds that shall burst on the morrow
    Be gathering above,
So dear in a year of sorrow
    Is a day of Love

What is Love but a Dreamer?

FLUTTERING, see, from the sunny wall
Shell-pink petals of roses fall,
Wavering on to the glassy stream ;
Softer than kisses given in dream
By lips that kiss not in waking day ;
Fairy boats, they are borne away ;
Airy fancies, that come not again ;
Lover's visions, that end in pain.

Well may Love wear wistful eyes !
Well may all love-words end in sighs !
What is Love but a dreamer—his dream
What but a rose-leaf dropped on a stream ?

The Song-Master

Know ye in the days of Spring,
When the new-leafed woodlands ring,
Some rich moment when a hush
Falls on the loud-throated thrush,
And the gold-mouthed blackbirds pour
Their Pactolian tides no more?

Rare, ah! rare the silence then!
For, unheard of dull-eared men,
Love himself, the Master's way,
Sings the birds to silence.—They,
Listening, learn, and after sing
Sweeter all the days of Spring.

The Herald-Flower

First Love is like the early daffodil
   That lightens the whole world with hope
      of Spring,
And sees not its own prophecies fulfil.

For when the leaves break forth and thrushes
      sing,
   The herald-flower is drooping. So the chill
Takes Love when he hath taught the heart
      to sing.

Lost Leaves of the Greek Anthology

HALCYON, by the gods' decree,
    For her love and sorrow's wage,
Nesteth in a summer sea,
    Though the winter round doth rage.

Since the gods love lovers so,
    They may jest at fortune's jars ;
Ports they have no pilots know,
    And in storm behold the stars.

From earthy crust
    The crystal core :
From livid rust
    The shining ore :

From natural lust,
    Refined thrice o'er,
Love the august
    Which gods adore.

A feeble hand can spoil the flowers
    That once were all the garden's joy :
And lives so bright as once were ours
    Are spoilt by Love—a little boy.

(*With a mirror*)

I send thee, love, for thy sole view,
A picture of my heart most true,
A portrait marvellous indeed,
A secret thou alone canst read,
For thou alone beholdest there
What always in my heart I bear.

So sweet is my love's name that all
    Seem, chancing in the ways
Another by this name to call,
    To crown her with full praise.

The lyre of Love I locked away,
 Its chords were bright and true.
Is not to-morrow as to-day,
 To sing Love's service due?

In rust and dust I turned the key
 To take again my lyre:
The tuneful shell was cracked, ah
 me!
 And broke each golden wire.

———

Woman is like the Sea, y-wis
That changes every hour, but is
The same through all the centuries.

Part III
Man's Love

In Inferno Sustulit Oculos

You—and I did not know !—
    Were in the world with me !
And nothing between us there
    But land and sea !

I played at love with women,
    I played at labour with men ;
You—and I did not know !—
    Were there all then.

Nothing of Heaven seemed certain,
    Nothing of Earth sublime ;
You—and I did not know !—
    There all the time.

You, with the angel wings,
    Who walk in heavenly light,
Whom the Great Gulf keeps from me
    In the fiery night.

In Exitu Amoris

Never a love to be loved again,
   Long as I live, by me!
What, if I drag awhile the chain?
   It is broken, and I am free.

Never a song to be sung again,
   When the woodland thrills with song,
And the primrose lightens the darkening lane
   As the April days grow long!

Never a dream to be dreamed again,
   When music softly plays,
And the soul breaks free from the tyrannous brain,
   And wanders in starry ways!

Never a heart to be hot again,
   Or a soul with itself at war!
Never a smile to be Heaven to gain,
   Or a face to be hungered for!

Cynthia

When she arose, as the maid-moon rises,
    Hallowing the darkened air,
A thousand silver and gold surprises
    Sprang round her everywhere.

The old worn world was a new strange world,
    Wonder and joy were there;
And my heart like a late-born flower unfurled
    That never had hope to be fair.

A Song of Farewell

FADE, vision bright!
   What clinging hands can stay thee?
Die, dream of light!
   What clasping hands can pray thee?
Farewell, delight!
   I have no more to say thee.

The gold was gold,
   The little while it lasted;
The dream was true,
   Although its joy be blasted;
That hour was mine,
   Although so swift it hasted.

A Love-Song

I HAVE no armour 'gainst thine eyes,
   When thou dost smile on me ;
Mine ears they are not enow wise
   To shut their doors to thee,
When, like the morn-arousing thrush,
Thou callest out of love's long hush.

The rain that from the sea arose,
   A vapour rare and free,
By clouds and springs and rivers goes
   Resistless to the sea.
And from the heart, hands, eyes of me
Love born of thee draws back to thee.

Omens and Dreams

THERE was a moaning in earth and air
   The day we parted,
And a wind went by like the breath
   of despair
   To the broken-hearted;
But little we dreamed of the coming
   pain,
As we murmured low, To meet again!

But a yellow sunset lit the West,
   And the snow-clad trees
Bowed to the leaden water's breast
   In the pitiless breeze.
Farewell, we said, Farewell for a day!
But the sad wind sighed, Farewell for
   aye!

The Afterglow

Here there is rain, and dead leaves whirling?
   I hear not, see not!—In my eyes
Is sunlight, in my ears the swirling
   Of snow-fed waters.—Which are lies?

So rich a glory streams about you,
   That one day with you shines afar,
Down through all darkened days without you,
   As through dull lamp-light shines a star.

Illumination

OTHER faces, yes,
   Have lent for me
A moment's loveliness
   To land and sea.

Thine has been as that
   One day of Spring,
When up the heart flies, at
   Heaven's gate to sing.

Visa Mihi Veritas

The light of Heaven, that fills all space
   In little stars doth shine ;
In miniature our souls embrace
   The measureless Divine.

And I have thought a girl's soft eyes
   And simple look might be
The very Truth of earth and skies
   Made visible to me.

The Word after Farewell

Not in the night of thy sorrow
   I fear thy forgetting;
But when the unmindful bright morrow
   Arise from this darkened day's setting,
Oh, let not thy heart put away
With its grief all the love of to-day!

In thine eyes, when thou smilest again,
   Let a softer light be,—
As the sun returns after the rain,—
   Remembering thy last smile on me;
And the roses of Love all thy years
Be bright with the pearls of past tears!

Together, Once

TOGETHER, once, in light of day
We stood, and I had leave to say
Whate'er I would. Ah, well-a-day!
   How could I speak of love?
My heart was happy as the bird
That soars and sings, and every word
Light as the summer air that stirred
   The summer leaves above.

Together, now, in dreams alone
I stand with thee; and now my tone
Is pleading as the marsh-wind's moan
   Beside the sad salt sea;
O love, I cry, for sweet Love's sake,
O love, reply to my heart's ache,
Or, love, I die!—And then I wake,
   And know thou'rt far from me.

Outre-Mer

If thou shouldst call across the sea,
I think thy voice would reach to me,
I think my heart would answer thee
    In thine extremest need.
Or if, laid deep in sepulchre,
Thou calledst me, I dare aver
The dust that was my heart should stir,
    The dust itself should bleed.

Or else, love, if it be not so,
What good thing has Love left to show,
What thing at all, when Fate says No
    To all we counted on?
A heart-prick in some wild-flower's
    scent:
A sting in places where we went:
A world all sand—all water spent—
    The morning mirage gone.

Kisses

THE wave, when the ship goes onward,
    Forgets the kiss of the keel;
And the wind, that the arrow startled,
    The keen sweet sting of the steel.

Are kisses so soon forgotten?
    Nay, what to you and me,
Who have walked in Eden together,
    Are tales of the wind and the sea!

Ask of the Nightingale

Ask of the nightingale
  A song, and she shall sing thee
Such falls as cannot fail
  Some inmost joy to bring thee.

But I, so fond, so fain,
  Am but as echo to thee,
That calls from walls again
  Thine own sweet name to woo
    thee.

A Song of Love

If in thine eyes
   I saw that softer light
That in the skies
   Doth herald Spring's delight,
Ah, love, how loud my heart should sing,
Ev'n as the blackbird to the Spring!

If on thy cheek
   I saw that warm hue play
That doth bespeak
   The dawn of a new day,
Ah, love, how like the lark should rise
My soul in rapture to the skies!

If from thy mouth
   I heard such whisper low
As from the South
   Doth through the pinewoods blow,
How should my whole soul murmur
     through
With music, as the pinewoods do!

A Silver Night

The silver shield of heaven all night
Defend thee, love, and be thy light;
And all the wakeful starry eyes
Keep watch above thee till day rise!

The idly wandering winds, that blow
Up to thy casement, thence shall go
More solemn with such joy to bear
Adown the silver-dusted air.

Till all the pine-tree tongues shall move
To syllable thy name of love,
And pass in whispers on to me
The wind-borne wonder-tale of thee.

Eheu, Fugaces!

THE wheels whirl faster year by year
Adown the slope of life ; I hear
The roaring of the Doom more near.

I catch at every flower that grows ;
I grasp the thorns and miss the rose ;
And life ungovernably goes.

O vision of an angel face,
That floatest nigh me for a space,
A dream of music and of grace !

I know not what thou art ; but bend
Thy soft eyes on me, and defend
From the fierce terror of the end !

A Summer Cloud

Yes, it was you,
The soft cloud in the summer blue,
So white, so warm,
That brought the thunder and the storm.

So warm, so white,
With broad rays like a ladder bright,
That reached to heaven,
The very highest of the seven.

Earth seemed as fair,
As crystalline the liquid air,
As painters drew
In Italy when Art was new.

Yes, it was you,
Transfigured earth awhile, then drew
The dreadful rain
That drowned a whole life's garnered gain.

A Fallen Idol

If Dante, when he steeled his soul
    To face the fires of Hell
By dreams of Beatrice—his goal
    The Heaven where she did dwell:

If, having lost the world for this,
    He, in the lowest Pit
Had found her whom he thought in Bliss,
    My fate and his would fit.

Any Man to any Woman

As some musk-breathing night of May
   When odorous dews grow rare
On flowers too glad to sleep away
   One hour of life so fair :

As some mid-winter night of pain,
   When every shivering tree
Grows ice-sheathed from the deadly
   rain—
   These hast thou been to me.

A Man's Question

Why did you snap the string,
When it was rendering
At your light touch its fullest sweetest
    tone ?
Did it not give its whole
Of music ? and its soul,
Was it not utterly and all your own ?

One moment—a low chord
Ringing with love's reward
And crownèd hope that trembled into
    peace ;
Then with light violence
You smote the string-strained tense
And bade for ever that soft voice to
    cease.

The Bird and the Beacon

Poor bird that battlest with the storm
    To gain the beacon-light,
Then fall'st a wounded woeful form
    Into the gulfs of night!
A thousand lips that light may bless:
To thee 'tis the last bitterness.

A light was given to the earth,
    Wearing a woman's name;
A thousand tongues have told her worth,
    And deathless is her fame.
But I was the spent bird, that there
Salvation sought, and found despair.

The Story of a Lover's Soul

Oh, the days of a dawning rapture
    In earth and skies,
When a callow soul came tame to the capture
    Of thy soft eyes;
When a fluttering heart to thy hand came meekly,
As a 'scaped cage-bird when the wind blows bleakly!

All my heart at thy kisses kindled,
    As a wine-fed flame;
All my old self was scorched and dwindled,
    As a new self came;
As a new self grew, like the tender grasses
In the blackened forest, when the fire passes.

Oh, the days of the revelation
    Of the glory of Love!
Earth itself was a new creation;
    And Heaven above,
Height beyond height, unreached, undreamed,
Wide open to my winged soul seemed.

Oh, the days of the desolation,
    The days of fire !
The darkened heavens--the desecration
    Of high desire !
When the heart, that was Love's Dodona, lies
A blackened desert where dust-whirls rise.

The Poisoned Butterfly

How should the butterfly divine,
    When on the lily's crest he lit,
How poisoned was her honey-wine,—
    How nevermore his wings would flit
Like flame among the woods of pine?

How should the butterfly have guessed,
    When in the lily's heart he lay,
'Nor ever folded to the nest,
    As blossoms fold at close of day,
How near the sun was to the West?

How should the butterfly have deemed
    The drowsiness that fell on him
Was more than when at noon he dreamed,
    Half drowsy, on the rose's brim—
So sweet, so mild his slumber seemed!

But I was such a butterfly,
    Who fluttered to a flower as fair,
Nor dreamed from such delight to fly,
    So sweetly poisoned was the snare:
Now, sick past help, she casts me by.

Finis sine Fine

The fires in ashes lie
That leapt so wildly high;
The last faint sparks are dying
   dying;
Nothing is left of love
But vapours ris'n above,
And ashes coldly lying.

Is this, is this the end?
O love, O life, O friend!
A raptured hour, a swift forgetting,
And earth for evermore
Lone as an island shore
Where breaks no wave but brings
   some old regretting?

The Happy Spring

The lark 'gan sing,
   The lamb was playing,
The happy Spring
   All hearts obeying.

And then I crept
   Where Love lay sleeping,
And wept, and wept,
   And still am weeping.

The One Day

In a labyrinthine woodland
   I met the Lady May,
Fresh with showers, sweet with
     flowers,
   And I followed all the day
Her footsteps in the long grass
   Where the dew was brushed away.

When the even fell she vanished,
   And the night came dark with
     rain ;
Through the woods the spirits
     banished
   Shrieked fitfully in pain ;
And I had lived the one day
   That in life comes not again.

The Magic Maiden

Is there poison on thy lips
   Magic maiden?
Like the luscious flowers death-laden
   The wild bee sips,
   In deep forest glooms,
   Whose stars are blooms.

Though mine eyes drank love at thine
   'Twas but pastime,
Till, alas! we met the last time;
   Thy lips touched mine.
   And now I draw to thee,
   Thou moon—I see.

A Magic Circle

Ah, halting oft is human speech,
    Darling, whose name is Love's for me ;
But as we sat upon the beach
No words we needed, each from each ;
    Such voices found we in the sea,
    And in the winds that wandered free.

What need to say *I love you*, when
    Your hair was blown about my face ?
While the sea's music seemed to pen
    A fold enchanted far from men
    (Such airy walls as wizards trace),
    To shut the world out from our place.

Oh, wonder of Love's supreme day !
    That light is faded long ago ;
The sea, and all the world, is gray ;
But that one spot of earth for aye
    Is ringed with magic radiance, though
    A thousand pass there and not know.

Earth has Forgotten

EARTH has forgotten
   Her Eden days,
And the garden hidden
   From human gaze,
The angel footsteps,
   The thornless ways.

O world unwitting!
   No spot of thee
But might in a moment
   All Eden be,
Could I have my lost love
   There with me!

Via Invia

Were any fain to reach a star,
   He would not fashion stairways high,
Seek foot by foot to climb so far,
   Or step by step ascend the sky.

Nay, he would scorn the eagle's wings,
   To dare an undiscovered way,
Leap out upon the night's blue rings,
   And hail at dawn his wished-for day.

I will not vainly seek to thee
   By ladder-steps of wealth or fame,
Till some few feet below me be
   The world—thy distance still the same.

Love's is an empire larger far
   Than land or sea or liquid air.
Though thou wert further than a star,
   Love easily should bring me there.

A Rondel of the Ivy-Leaf

The ivy-leaf she loves to wear
   In token of Fidelity;
   For ever-green's the ivy tree,
And she's as faithful as she's fair.

Yet scarce my breaking heart can bear
   For ever at her breast to see
The ivy-leaf she loves to wear
   In token of Fidelity.

Were she less faithful or less fair!
   O Love, forgive the blasphemy!
   But since her love is not for me
To me 'tis token of Despair,
The ivy-leaf she loves to wear.

A Rondel of Absence

When my dear lady is away,
  Her lightest word is then my law ;
  As wayward sands, when tides withdraw,
Repeat the wavelets' lightest play.

Though daily I should disobey
  When she is by, and show no awe,
When my dear lady is away,
  Her lightest word is then my law.

Fierce as a flagellant I flay
  My own back for the slightest flaw,
  That she would pardon if she saw :
I pardon nothing in that day
When my dear lady is away.

Love Sonnets. I

From woods, from mountains, and from lonely streams,
  But most from fair girl-faces I have drawn
The inspiration which in after dreams
  Floods all the spirit, like a golden dawn.
  But now to be half-human, as a Faun,
Or more than human, as an Angel, seems
Alone desirable ; whom fancy deems
  Awake to beauty, but from love withdrawn.
For on thy loveliness if I could gaze
  And feel, not human love, but that desire,
  Spirit exalting, which the stars inspire
On summer nights or seas on summer days :
  Then might I read, writ clear in human eyes,
  The undeciphered speech of seas and skies.

Love Sonnets. II

Thy face should be a Tintoret's despair;
  Nor Raphael nor Leonardo could,
  Limning thy beauty on their lifeless wood,
Reveal thyself that art chief beauty there.
  Though all the world before thy picture stood,
And called it beautiful beyond compare,
  I only might stand by in bitter mood,
Searching that fair face for the self more fair.

Swift clouds they paint, winds blowing, seas in madness,
  The lightning's flashing, and the rainbow's sheen;
    Thee may they paint, as some men see and hear thee;
But who can give the glory, who the gladness,
  The hope, the sanctity, that is not seen,
    But streams into my soul when I am near thee?

Love Sonnets. III

Now hath the ageing year forgot thee, June,
  And doteth on the Mœnad month, October;
How harlot-like she wastes his wealth ! How soon
  His gold shall all be gone, and he left sober !
Yet can I not forget thy days of swoon,
  Dear June, at Henley ; though the daft disrober
Beat' his leaf-tatters all the afternoon
  About me, playing mad to please October.

Still seems the dull day must be brighter there,
  The trees full-leafed, the meadow-grass full green ;
    While Thames, here turbid, there steals softly on
A dream of silver, her light boat to bear.
  Yet well I know how changed is that fair scene :
    Or hides it in some mystic Avalon ?

Love Sonnets. IV

And all my dream of her—is that but dreaming?
  Was it not heaven at her side to be?
Or this too, is it as a mirage gleaming,
  A desert that, looked back on, seems a sea?
A desert, that day? Nay then, what redeeming
  Hath this day?—Speak, dull memory! Was not she
The vision of the Grail, all heaven streaming
  About her, for all white souls, and for me?

Not so: though now a light is on those hours,
  Most were not golden that I had with her,
    Many were maddened.—Peace! my dream is now
More true than memory; 'tis a dream of flowers;
  That was a day of flowers: no wind did stir,
    And I was with her 'neath the willow-bough.

Love Sonnets.   V

I wake from one more Circe-draught of love,
  And all my soul is sick with sulphur fumes
And poisonous salt savours.   Yet, above
  The   noisome   hell-reek   that   my   soul
    consumes,
The blood-taste and the blackness, I am 'ware
  Of some o'erwhelming terror that before
O'ertook me not in my most dark despair ;
  A cold wind drives me to some dreadful
    door.

Death is it ?   I have long been friends with
    Death.
  Hell is it ?   I have oft been housed in Hell.
It is not Madness, though it maddeneth,
  Nor fanged Remorse—I know Remorse
    too well.
What, Love ! were those but flittings, this thy
    flying ?
What, Love ! were those thy slumbers, this
    thy dying ?

Part IV
Maiden's Love

The Story of the Rose

The rose said, Yes!
  And the butterfly—
Ah, you may guess
  His ecstasy!
How like a kiss his wing-plumes brushed
Her petals, and how fair she blushed.

The rose said, Stay!
  But another rose
Beside bloomed gay:
  The bright wings rose,
Across the upturned face they cast
A moment's shadow, and then passed.

But ere the bird
  Of night was calling,
Unseen, unheard,
  Were petals falling,
Like drops in caverns, leaf by leaf,
Done with life, and love, and grief.

To-day He Loves Me

To-day he loves me!—Time, stand still!
Haste not, sun, behind the hill!
To-day he loves me: no to-morrow
Can touch this one to-day with sorrow.

As a crystal well o'erspills
With sweet water from the hills,
So my heart o'erbrims with blisses,
Of looks, of love-words, and of kisses.

And through many a day of drought
Love shall come to draw thereout,
Singing low—though this to-day
Be then a year-old yesterday—
"To-day he loves me!" ('Tis Love's way).

"Si vous croyez que je vais dire."

    My lips must say not,
    My eyes betray not
      My heart's hid treasure ;
    My hands must deaden,
    My feet go leaden,
      Not leap in measure.

    For how they would rate me,
    Preach me and prate me,
      Scoff at and scold me,
    Should they discover
    Who is my lover,
      And what he has told me !

Ce que vivent les Roses.

The stream, that flows for ever,
  Whispered to the daffodil,
" Would you not be as the river,
  Ever living, ever flowing,
  Never fading, never knowing
    Death the chill?"

But the daffodil made answer,
  " I have lived one day of Spring,
When the wind with me was dancer;—
  Oh, the brightness! Oh, the fleet-
    ness!
  Oh, the rapture! What more sweet-
    ness
      Could life bring?"

I and You

Man differeth from man, as leaf from leaf,
    As star from star;
And ev'n the hearts that suffer the same grief
    Are parted far.

And ev'n the souls, that through the windows gaze
    Of wistful eyes,
Are aureoled each for each, as by the haze
    Of wintry skies.

A Woman's Question

Why do you love me so well?
    I am only a woman :
No angel from Heaven or Hell,
    But earthly and human.

And you—by your eyes' flame I see,
    By your heart-beat I know it,
Have dreamed me a Beatrice—me,
    You Dante, my poet.

Shall I yield you my soul-stuff to be
    Your soul-fire's fuel?
There is that would take fire in me,
    But were it not cruel

To feed for one hour a fire,
    How sacred soever?
Then see my delight, your desire,
    In ashes for ever?

Not in Naxos

An August day—a sky o'ercast—
   A gray Down sloping to the sea—
A sea like a face where death has passed,
   Motionless but for misery.
Hardly a breath in the heavy air,
   Hardly a wave on the heaving tide ;
The very pebbles were silent there,
Chatterers stilled by the great despair.
   No voice was there, nor sound, beside
   A faint dull moaning that rose and died,
   The mere heart-beat of the ocean wide.
Above was the waste Down, bare and blind,
The dancing place of the winter wind ;
Now silent and lone as the wan lamps show
The dancing rooms when the dancers go.

Half-way down, from the cliff-face lent
A tower of chalk, like a battlement,
With a crest of waving grass, like hair.
Motionless sat a maiden there ;
Her locks streamed loose, her lips were pale :
Her eyes were fixed on a far-off sail.

An old-world story, a far-off woe,
Made beautiful by its long ago?
Nay, 'tis a different story this!
Yet on her lips is her lover's kiss;
Yet in her heart is the agony;
For this was yesterday, and I,
Who tell it you in the talk of men
I was the Ariadne then.

A Story heard on a Violin

She loved. Her whole heart grew around
A baser nature, which it bound
With beauty, as the purple vine,
Which makes the stone or stem divine.

She lost. His grosser nature woke
And from her glorious bondage broke;
And she was left, a plant forlorn,
With drooping leaves and tendrils torn.

Know ye the maiden?—I have met
One like her. In her eyes lay yet
The pain. From viol-strings she drew
A human cry that thrilled me through.

A Revolt

PALE and passionless star,
Steadily wheeling afar
 From the golden Sun, thy lord!
What is thy love's reward?
Cycles ever the same,
Timeless, tireless, tame.

Rather be my love's fashion
The fiery meteor's passion,
 That scorns the planet's orbit,
  And ever flies to the Sun,
Till its glorious lover absorb it,
  And life ends when love is won.

Planctus Displicentis

Why was I not born fair?
Not as world-famous Helen, past compare,
Drawing all hearts and eyes
To madness or magnificent emprise:

But as some village maid,
Chosen May-queen beneath the hawthorn shade,
Not fair enough to move
All women's jealousy, but one man's love.

INDEX TO FIRST LINES

	PAGE
A dream of light!—	39
A feeble hand can spoil the flowers	50
Ah, halting oft is human speech	84
An August day—a sky o'ercast—	103
And all my dream of her—is that but dreaming?	92
Art thou, poor wave-beat hull, the same	27
Ask of the nightingale	68
As some musk-breathing night of May	74
Bright is that wave of night	34
Dear is the sunny between-while	45
Earth has forgotten	85
Fade, vision bright!	58
First love is like the early daffodil	48
Fluttering, see, from the sunny wall	46
From earthy crust	49
From woods, from mountains, and from lonely streams	89
Halcyon, by the gods' decree	49
Here there is rain, and dead leaves whirling?	61

	PAGE
How lightly waver down through slanting beams	41
How should the butterfly divine	79
If Dante, when he steeled his soul	73
If in thine eyes	69
If thou shouldst call across the sea	66
I have no armour 'gainst thine eyes	59
I met Queen Spring in the Hanger	13
In a labyrinthine woodland	82
I saw one crouching in a place of gloom	29
I send thee, love, for thy sole view	50
Is there poison on thy lips?	83
I wake from one more Circe-draught of love	93
Know ye in the days of Spring	47
Lay by, sweet woodlands, your array	17
Love drinks our young sorrows up	37
Man differeth from man, as leaf from leaf	101
Most strange it is to stand when shades are free	28
My lips must say not	99
Never a love to be loved again	56
Not from all shells in Indian bays	35
Not in the night of thy sorrow	64
Now hath the ageing year forgot thee, June	91
O heart, what boots thy wild wing-beating	2
Oh, the days of a dawning rapture	77
Oh, the Maytime	15
O little singing bird	12

	PAGE
Other faces, yes . . .	62
O toilers of the day!	23
Pale and passionless star . . .	106
Poor bird that battlest with the storm . .	76
Roses drop their petals all around . .	16
Sands, forsaken, keep	38
She loved. Her whole heart grew around	105
Skimming an idle stone along the lake .	11
So sweet is my love's name, that all . . .	50
The doors of Eden close . . .	10
The fires in ashes lie	80
The heaven has emptied all her stars . .	33
The ivy-leaf she loves to wear . . .	87
The lark 'gan sing	81
The light of Heaven, that fills all space .	63
The lyre of Love I locked away . . .	51
There is a little plant that weaves . .	19
There was a moaning in earth and air . .	60
The rose said, Yes!	97
These little crawling ants for one day's space .	24
The sigh of the seawind wakes not . .	21
The silver shield of heaven all night . .	70
The storm is dying with the day . . .	22
The stream, that flows for ever . . .	100
The sweetest words that tongue has said . .	36
The wave, when the ship goes onward . .	67

	PAGE
The wheels whirl faster year by year	71
The wind blows warm from Italy	40
This is not Shelley—this dead mask of Death!	3
This is the grave of Love	42
Though joy and grief and pain	20
Thy face should be a Tintoret's despair	90
To-day he loves me!—Time, stand still!	98
Together, once, in light of day	65
Were any fain to reach a star	86
What shipmen steering by yon star	25
What wonder if, when Love awakes	44
When my dear lady is away	88
When she arose, as the maid-moon rises	57
When the night-wind stirs the pine	43
When woods are gold and hedges gay	18
Why did you snap the string	75
Why do you love me so well?	102
Why was I not born fair?	107
Wisdom to others—to see	8
Woman is like the Sea, y-wis	51
Yes, it was you	72
You—and I did not know!—	55

www.ingramcontent.com/pod-product-compliance
Lightning Source LLC
Chambersburg PA
CBHW020125170426
43199CB00009B/638